All Kinds of Trucks

Focus: Information

**PETER SLOAN &
SHERYL SLOAN**

This truck
carries cattle.

This truck
carries garbage.

This truck
carries concrete.

This truck
carries gas.

This truck
carries milk.

This truck
carries cars.

This truck
carries logs.